D0579313

CARNIVAL

Clare Chandler

WAYLAND

CHINESE NEW YEAR

CHRISTMAS

DIWALI

ID-UL-FITR

PASSOVER

Editor: Alison Cooper
Series editor: Sarah Doughty
Designer: Tim Mayer

First published in 1997 by Wayland Publishers Ltd
61 Western Road, Hove, East Sussex, BN3 1JD

British Library Cataloguing in Publication Data
Chandler, Clare
Carnival. - (Festivals)
1. Carnival - Juvenile literature
I. Title
394.2' 5

ISBN 0 7502 1940 8

Printed and bound by L.E.G.O. S. p. A., Vicenza, Italy

Picture acknowledgements
Britstock 6 (Eric Bach), 14 bottom (Bernd Ducke); J Allan Cash 29; Cephas 11 bottom (Nigel Blythe); ET Archive 10; Mary Evans 8, 9 top, 11 top; Robert Harding cover centre top, 4 centre (Roy Rainford), 5 top left (Charles Bowman), 7 (Tomlinson), 16 top, 23 top (Roy Rainford), 24 bottom; Life File 4 top (Andrew Ward), 23 bottom (Andrew Ward); Photri cover top left and 15 (Scott Berne); Tony Stone Worldwide cover centre (Ary Diesendruck), title page (Doug Armand), 5 right (Doug Armand), 5 bottom left (Aldo Torelli), 16-17 (Oliver Benn), 18-19 (Aldo Torelli), 20 (Ary Diesendruck), 21 (Aldo Torelli), 22 (Doug Armand), 26 (Fred Wood), 28 (Craig Wells); Ville de Nice 27; Wayland Picture Library 12 (Zak Waters), 29 (Tim Woodcock); Zefa cover bottom left (Bertsch), bottom centre, 4 bottom (B. Benjamin), 13 (Lothar Schroter), 14 top (B. Benjamin), 24 top (T. Schneiders), 25 (Bertsch). Artwork by Tim Mayer.

CONTENTS

CARNIVAL AROUND THE WORLD

The Notting Hill Carnival in London takes place in August rather than in February, as there is a better chance of fine weather.

The people of Venice dress up in Renaissance costume for their Carnival. During the Renaissance in the fifteenth and sixteenth centuries, Venice was a very important city.

Bands of pipers parade in the famous Carnival processions of Basle in Switzerland.

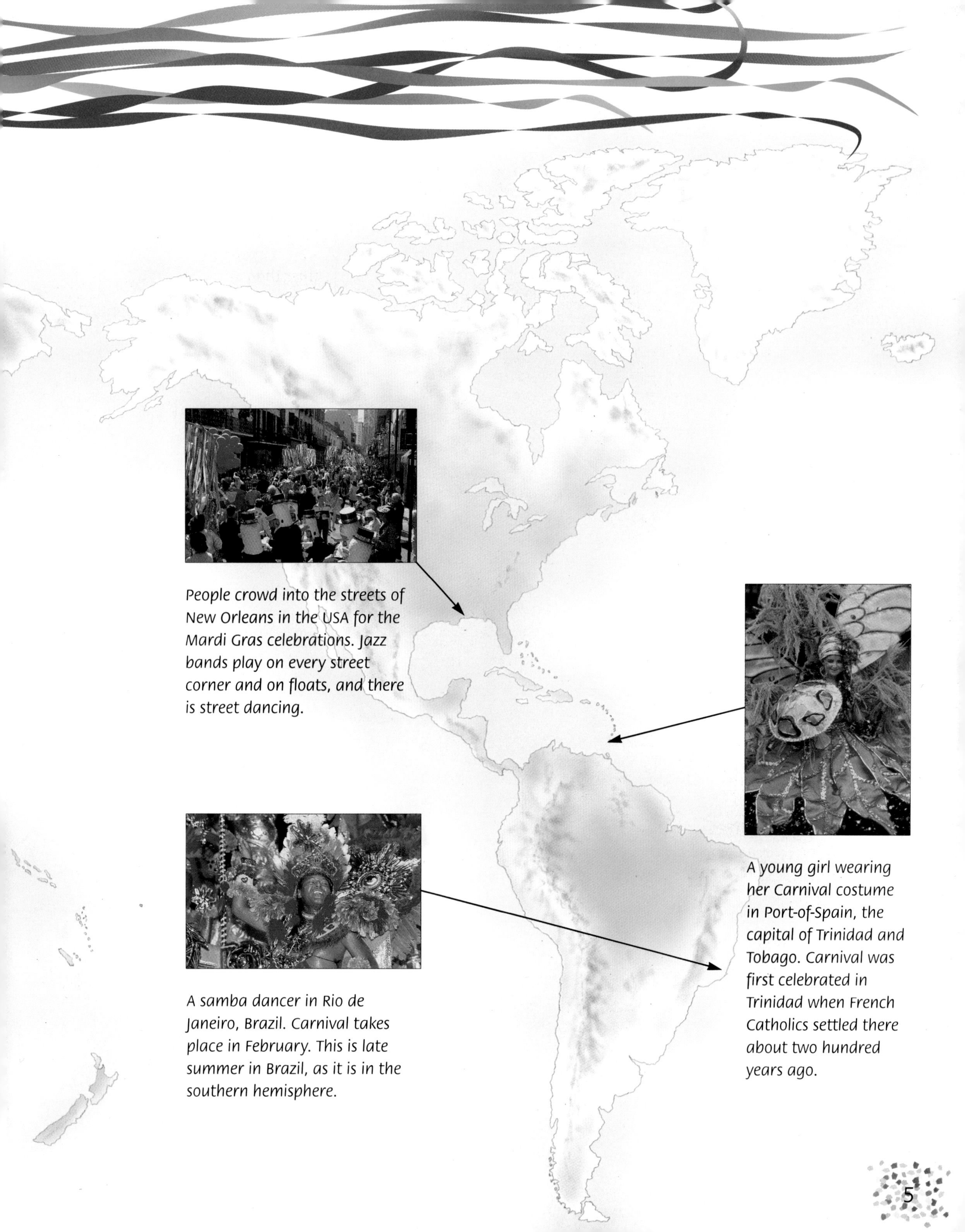

People crowd into the streets of New Orleans in the USA for the Mardi Gras celebrations. Jazz bands play on every street corner and on floats, and there is street dancing.

A young girl wearing her Carnival costume in Port-of-Spain, the capital of Trinidad and Tobago. Carnival was first celebrated in Trinidad when French Catholics settled there about two hundred years ago.

A samba dancer in Rio de Janeiro, Brazil. Carnival takes place in February. This is late summer in Brazil, as it is in the southern hemisphere.

CARNIVAL TIME!

Carnival is a wild and happy festival. All over the world, cities come alive as people take time off work and school to enjoy the celebrations. Night and day the air hums with the sounds of music and it is fragrant with the smells of special food cooking. During the day the streets are full of people parading in costumes, and in the evening the parties begin.

Dancers enjoying Carnival in Rio de Janeiro, Brazil. The festival is the highlight of the year for many of the people who live there.

Originally, Carnival was celebrated in countries where Roman Catholicism was the main faith. It has been spread all over the world by emigrants who have taken their customs to their new countries.

THE BATTLE OF FLOWERS

Throwing flowers and leaves is an ancient custom that is supposed to bring good luck, like throwing confetti at a wedding. Many Carnivals end in a shower of petals as people throw flowers at each other. One of the most famous flower battles is the Tournament of Roses held at Pasadena, California, in the USA.

In most countries, Carnival takes place in February. It marks the beginning of the season of Lent, the most solemn time of the Christian year. During this period, Christians remember the time that Jesus spent alone in the desert, preparing himself for his work of teaching and preaching. Traditionally, Lent was a time of fasting, or at least a period when only very simple foods were eaten. The name 'Carnival' comes from the Latin words *carne vale*, which mean 'farewell to meat'.

Before the serious forty days of Lent begin, Christians allow themselves a few days of fun. In many places Carnival lasts strictly for two days, but in other countries it continues for three days or more. Everywhere, though, the preparations for the festival begin many months beforehand.

A lot of time and effort goes into preparing huge floats for the processions. This one is in Nice in the south of France.

THE HISTORY OF CARNIVAL

There are many ways of celebrating Carnival, and some of these customs began a very long time ago. Although Carnival is a Christian festival, it developed originally from the winter festivals that people celebrated long before Christianity began.

THE BATTLE OF SUMMER AND WINTER

Some Carnival traditions are about new life and fertility, and they have ancient origins. During the Middle Ages, an event called the Battle of Summer and Winter was held all over Europe. Actors playing the parts of Summer and Winter staged a fight in which Summer conquered Winter. People believed that this would make sure that spring would arrive, bringing with it the growth of the next year's crops. At the end of the battle, sheaves of corn were buried. This was called 'burying the carnival'.

This medieval scene shows a mock battle similar to the Battle of Summer and Winter. Here Spring and his supporters (right) have triumphed over the miserable figure of Winter on the left.

This seventeenth-century painting by Pieter Bruegel shows an ancient German Carnival custom.

One of these ancient festivals was celebrated by the Romans and called Saturnalia. Saturn was their god of the harvest. In the deepest part of winter, they held the festival of Saturnalia to honour him and to encourage spring to return. The festival was a public holiday that lasted for a week. There was feasting and wild merrymaking, and for just one day slaves and their owners changed places. The slaves wore their owners' clothes and had their meals served to them by their masters. The Romans really enjoyed Saturnalia, so when Christianity became the official religion of the Romans, the Christian leaders decided it would be better to let the festival continue. But it was only allowed for two days just before Lent.

The Spanish converted many of the people of South America to Christianity. This sixteenth-century picture shows native Mexicans taking Communion.

Carnival is celebrated most in countries where the main faith is Roman Catholicism. From the sixteenth century, explorers from Roman Catholic countries such as Spain and France settled in other countries. There, they continued to practise their religion, and many native people were converted to Christianity. Christian customs soon became widespread. Carnival, for example, was taken to South America by Spanish settlers and to the West Indies by the French.

The European settlers in the Caribbean brought thousands of Africans to work as slaves on their sugar plantations. The slaves adopted the festival of Carnival, and their African traditions influenced the music, dance, costume and food.

When slavery was finally abolished, Carnival was a good time for the slaves to celebrate their freedom. This is still an important part of the festival in many areas – it is a few days in the year when people cast off the chains of authority and are free to enjoy themselves as they please.

SLAVERY

At the beginning of the seventeenth century, Europeans began the terrible trade in human life that was known as the slave trade. Having captured people in Africa, the Europeans shipped them to the Americas and sold them there as slaves. This trade continued for over two hundred years. Slavery was not abolished in the USA until the middle of the nineteenth century.

Above: People who used to be slaves celebrate their new freedom on Barbados in 1834.

Since the 1950s, many Afro-Caribbeans have left the West Indies and gone to live in other countries. Where they have settled in large numbers, they have carried on their tradition of Carnival. In places where the winters are cold, they celebrate Carnival in the summer. London's Notting Hill Carnival and the Caribana of Toronto are celebrated in August.

West Indians who have made their homes in London celebrate Carnival in the traditional way.

FESTIVE FOOD

In the beginning, Carnival was a preparation for the Christian season of Lent, the forty days before Easter, when people ate only simple foods. Carnival was seen as a last chance to eat rich food, and that tradition has remained.

The main events of Carnival have always taken place on the day before Lent begins – Shrove Tuesday. This celebration is often called Mardi Gras, which is French for 'Fat Tuesday'. It gets its name because, traditionally, it was the day when people ate up all their fatty, rich foods before the Lent fast.

In Britain, people eat pancakes on Shrove Tuesday, because in the past it was a good way of using up all the eggs, milk and flour in the house. In some towns, they hold pancake races, in which people have to run while tossing a pancake in the air and catching it.

In Britain, pancakes are traditionally eaten on Shrove Tuesday. Tossing them whilst cooking is traditional, too!

Pretzels hanging from a stall in Germany. These are a favourite Carnival food.

On the Sunday before Lent begins, there is a procession called Boeuf Gras (which means 'Fat Cow') in parts of France. Butchers wearing fancy costumes lead cattle through the streets. Sometimes, there are people dressed up in cow costumes, along with the real animals!

Doughnuts are a popular Carnival treat in many parts of Europe. In Germany they also eat crisp, knot-shaped biscuits called pretzels. They like to eat pretzels with beer, and beer festivals where all the different brews can be sampled are also part of the celebrations.

At Carnival parties all over the world, there are all sorts of other drinks flowing. Street stalls sell tasty local delicacies such as hot spicy fritters or coconut cakes.

MUSIC

Music is an essential part of Carnival, and different styles of music are associated with the festival in different parts of the world. The West Indies are famous for their steel bands, and New Orleans, in the USA, is well known for its jazz. The street dancing in Spain is accompanied by castanets and guitars. In Brazil, samba bands weave in and out of the dancing crowds on the streets, with someone at the front blowing a whistle to warn people to keep out of the way.

Above: In Germany and Switzerland, bands of musicians, like this one in Basle, are a common sight at Carnival.

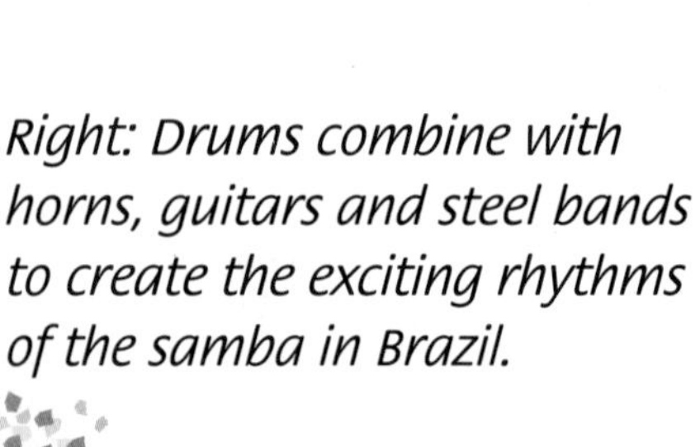

Right: Drums combine with horns, guitars and steel bands to create the exciting rhythms of the samba in Brazil.

In New Orleans, people started celebrating Carnival, or Mardi Gras, in 1827, when French students settled there. At that time, black slaves in New Orleans were only allowed to sing and dance together in a certain field on Sundays. In the mid-1800s, there were slave rebellions, and from then on the Sunday gatherings were banned. Slaves were only allowed to enjoy themselves together during Mardi Gras. Later, when slavery was finally ended, the festival became a time for them to celebrate their freedom.

Jazz players help to produce a lively atmosphere in New Orleans during Mardi Gras.

New Orleans was the birthplace of jazz. This music developed out of black American folk music and became linked with the black people's struggle for freedom. Its unusual rhythms make jazz just the right music for the unruly festival of Carnival. Nowadays, jazz bands play on every street corner of New Orleans, as well as on the floats that parade through the streets.

In the West Indies, Carnival was at first only celebrated by white people – the slaves were not allowed to join in. But as soon as slavery ended there in 1833, the newly-freed slaves took part in the festivities, bringing a strong African element to the rhythm of the music and dances. The music was so exciting and powerful that the European rulers were afraid the black population would get out of control, and so they banned drumming.

Above: A band in St Lucia makes joyful music out of old tins and hollowed-out bamboo stems.

The black people then invented another way of making music. They made percussion instruments out of dried and hollowed-out bamboo stems, which they either clapped together or banged on the ground. With these simple instruments, the Tamboo-bamboo bands, as they were called, were able to make loud, joyful music. Once again, the government feared that the excitement created by the music would lead to riots. Tamboo-bamboo music was banned in 1920.

Each dent in a steel drum makes a distinct sound. The melody pans, known as ping pongs, can produce thirty-two different notes.

WINSTON 'SPREE' SIMON AND THE STEEL BAND

Steel bands are said to have been invented in Trinidad by Winston 'Spree' Simon in the 1940s. The story goes that he was trying to hammer out the dents in his dustbin one day when he noticed that each blow of his hammer was making a different sound. He recognized some of the sounds as musical notes. He was so excited that he carried on making more dents in his dustbin until he had made all the notes in the musical scale. That was the beginning of the steel band.

The people could not be kept quiet for long, however. Soon they were making music out of old buckets, biscuit tins and other scrap metal, and this eventually led to the creation of steel bands. These are now an important part of Carnival, not just in the West Indies but in many other parts of the world.

SONG AND DANCE

Carnival is all about getting out and having fun. In cities all over the world, during Carnival time, there are people out on the streets, dancing and singing together. In some places, the songs and the dancing are a vital part of the festival.

Calypsos are special songs that originated in the West Indies. They have catchy rhythms and tunes, but the words are the most important part. They have all sorts of themes – some are about love or other personal themes, others are about local issues. Often, they are critical of politics or people in power, but although calypsos can be insulting, they are always good-humoured.

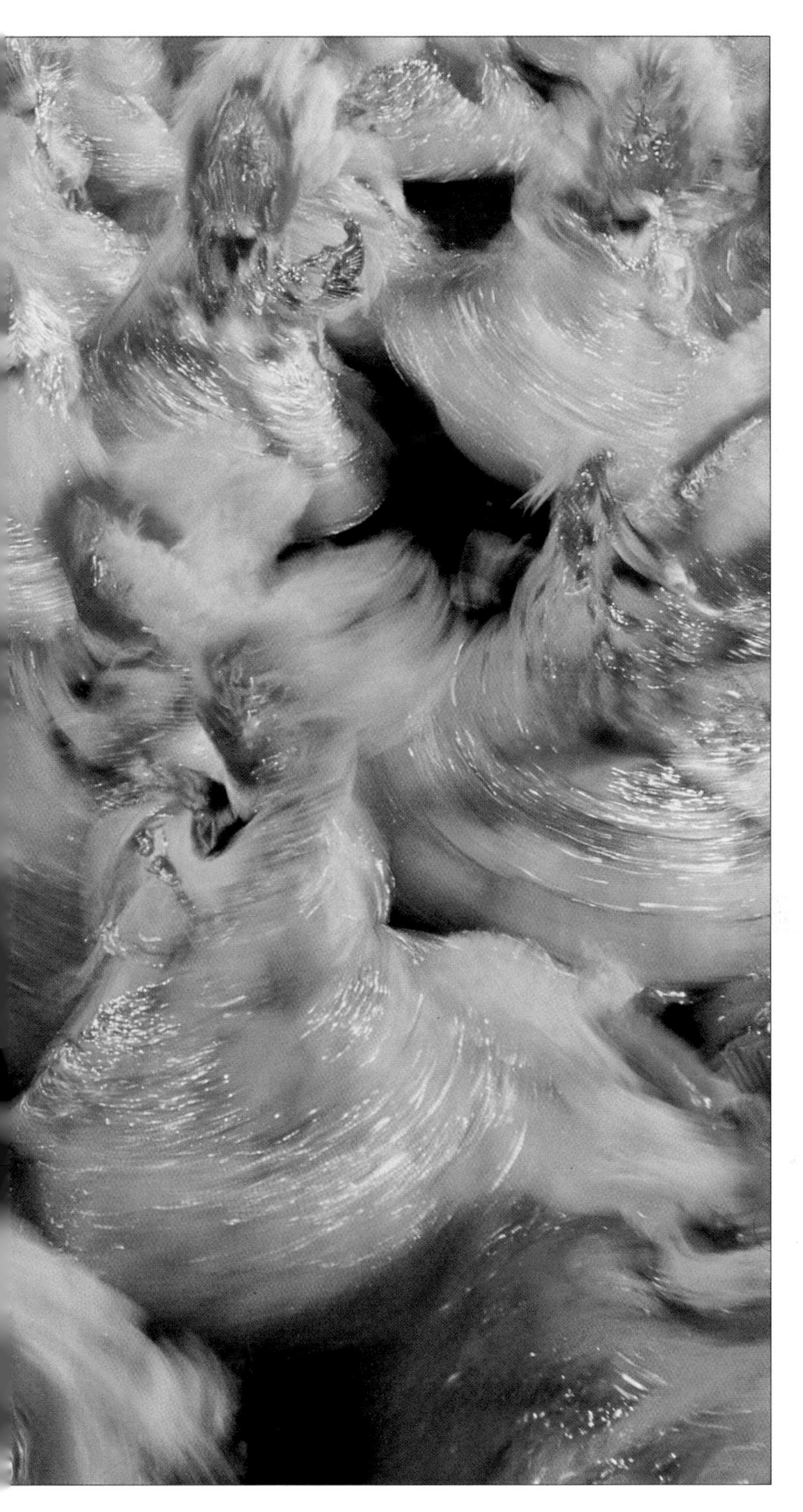

The songs are performed every night in Carnival 'tents', which are actually often halls or other large buildings. The success of each calypso is judged by the enthusiasm of the audience. If the audience do not like the song, then they will jeer the singer off the stage with slow hand-clapping. The most popular calypso every year becomes the Carnival theme and the singer, or calypsonian, is crowned 'Calypso King' or 'Queen'. The calypsonians dress in amazing costumes and call themselves names such as 'Mighty Sparrow', 'Sir Lancelot' or 'Calypso Rose'.

The rhythm of calypso is African and the word 'calypso' is thought to come from the West African word 'kaiso'. This has a similar meaning to the English word 'bravo' and it is still shouted by audiences in appreciation of a good calypso.

A lot of care goes into the planning of spectacular, whirling dances, like this one in Rio de Janeiro, Brazil.

Many people were taken from Africa to Brazil to work as slaves, and so here, too, the African influence is very strong. It can be seen in the strong rhythms and movements of their traditional Carnival music and dance – the samba. Four of Brazil's major cities, Rio de Janeiro, Salvador, Recife and São Paulo, have big Carnival celebrations, but Rio's is the most spectacular of them all. The city is divided into 'schools' that compete with each other to create the most fabulous floats and costumes. They are judged on their music and dancing as well as on their display.

The African influence on the celebrations in Brazil can be seen in the decorations on this huge float.

Carnival in Europe tends to be less exuberant, probably because it takes place in colder weather, but there is often street dancing. In Germany and Switzerland, groups of singers go from house to house, rather like carol singers at Christmas.

Extravagant, colourful costumes combine with the rhythms of the samba to make a fantastic party atmosphere.

SAMBA SONG

Sambalele was downhearted,
For him the day had not started.
Sambalele was not playing,
He could not see people swaying.

Samba samba samba olé!
Hear how the music is swinging away.
Samba samba samba olé!
Now you'll be happy dancing all day.

Sambalele started sighing,
As on his bed he was lying,
Sambalele heard the flurry,
Then up he jumped in a hurry.

Sambalele started dancing,
Soon he was swaying and prancing,
Sambalele friends he's bringing,
And soon they're all gaily singing.

COSTUME

An important part of every Carnival is dressing up. It is called 'playing mask', from the French word *masquerade*, meaning a fancy dress ball. Everyone who takes part in the celebrations parades in wonderful costumes that are as exotic and colourful as possible.

Costumes worn by children are just as beautiful and elaborate as those worn by adults.

In countries such as Brazil where Carnival is taken very seriously, people spend all year designing and making the wonderful costumes. The samba 'schools' may have thousands of members, masqueraders and musicians who will all need costumes! This takes thousands of metres of beautiful material. Often, the costumes are so elaborate that the people wearing them hardly dare move to avoid spoiling the effect. Each school chooses a 'Queen', who wears the most fabulous costume of all and stands on a float built especially for the Carnival.

Above: The Venice Carnival is famous for its spectacular costumes and masks.

Below: All sorts of unusual materials are used to make the costumes. This one is made of straw.

Often, the costumes are related to the history of the city. For example, in Venice a stunning procession of Venetians parades to St Mark's Square in the centre of the city. Their costumes are copies of clothes from the Renaissance period of history, during the fifteenth and sixteenth centuries, when Venice was a very important city.

At the Mardi Gras celebrations in New Orleans, USA, many people wear costumes that are similar to those worn by men and women who lived there at the end of the nineteenth century.

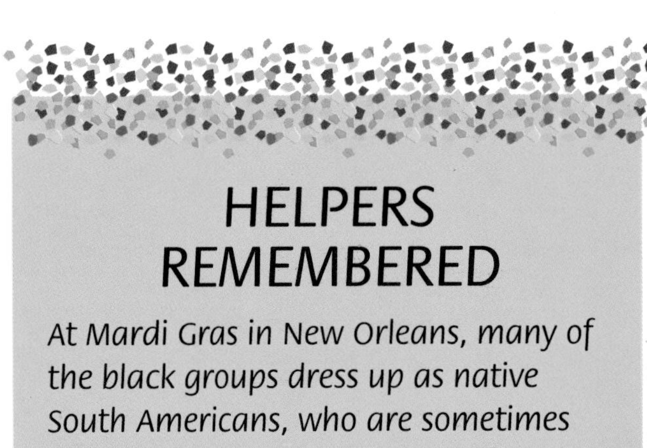

HELPERS REMEMBERED

At Mardi Gras in New Orleans, many of the black groups dress up as native South Americans, who are sometimes called Indians. This is because after the slave rebellions in the nineteenth century, many native South Americans helped the slaves by sheltering those who had run away.

MASKS AND DISGUISES

Part of the fun of Carnival is the chance to become someone different for a few days. Many people take the opportunity to put on a mask with their costume and be in disguise during the festivities. This gives them the freedom to do and say things they would not normally do.

The traditional Carnival figures of witches, ghosts and devils appear in almost every procession, but each country has some special disguises of its own. These can be quite scary. In Austria, along with the witches and ghosts, figures representing death parade the streets to the music of drums, whips and bull-roarers. In other parts of Europe, groups of masked actors go from house to house, performing plays.

Above: A parade in a town in southern Germany. The costumes and masks are often passed down from one generation to another.

Right: Masked dancers on the island of Barbados.

When Carnival first arrived in Trinidad, only white people were allowed to take part. Many of them would dress up as slaves. After slavery was ended in 1833, Carnival became a celebration for the newly-freed black people. Many of them chose to dress in the finery of their former European owners, sometimes with white masks. Nowadays, though, people dress up as all sorts of characters, from traditional African figures to Scottish Highlanders.

Many Carnival processions include people walking on stilts. These people are taking part in the celebrations in the British Virgin Islands.

Some people like to take on the character of the figure they are representing and will practise for days beforehand. Sometimes they parade the same costume each year and eventually become known as that character. Masqueraders have an old custom of visiting friends' houses to see how long it takes for them to be recognized.

CARNIVAL CHARACTERS

There are some traditional characters who have been part of the West Indian Carnival for a long time. Moco Jumbie is a figure from West African folklore who parades the streets on stilts, wearing a long skirt, a satin jacket and an admiral's hat decorated with feathers. Borroquites is a masquerader who seems to be riding a horse. The horse's head is made from a bamboo framework and attached to the front of the masquerader. Jab Molassi means the Molasses Devil. He is covered with molasses or black paint and carries a long whip. He prances through the streets threatening to smear black paint over any onlookers who do not give him money.

GIANTS

Huge giants are a feature of many Carnival processions. Enormous figures representing historical, mythical and magic characters are made especially for the festival every year and carried through the streets.

Carnival parades in the German towns of Munich and Cologne include giants, but the most famous giants are those in Spain. In Valencia and Pamplona, they have spectacular Carnival celebrations, in which elaborate sculptures made from papier-mâché and figures with enormous heads parade through the towns. These originally represented the traditional theme of the Battle of Summer and Winter, but nowadays they are almost always historical figures. Some of the processions have figures of King Ferdinand and Queen Isabella of Spain, who united their country against Moorish invaders and finally drove them out in 1492. Other people in the processions dress as Moors and sometimes a mock battle is staged between the two groups.

Giant figures can be seen at many Carnival celebrations. This figure of a native South American is typical of the Mardi Gras procession in New Orleans.

On the island of Haiti in the West Indies, the Carnival figures represent African gods and important historical figures, such as Toussaint L'Ouverture. He is the national hero who in 1804 established the first republic in the world to be led by black people.

In the south of France, Mardi Gras is led by a huge straw man – the King of the Carnival. He heads a procession, bright with flowers, of floats, clowns and horses.

This float, with its enormous Chinese figures and dragon, is one of many which take part in parades in France.

THE CHRISTIAN CALENDAR

Advent December
The Christian Church begins its year in December with the season of Advent. It lasts just over three weeks and it is the time when people prepare for Christmas. Many children have Advent calendars which have 24 or 25 windows to open. They open a window each day to see the picture inside.

Christmas December
Christmas is the festival when Jesus Christ's birth is celebrated. It lasts for 12 days. Christmas Day is on 25 December, although Orthodox Christians celebrate Christmas on 6 January. ▼

Epiphany 6 January
Epiphany is the last of the 12 days of Christmas. Epiphany means 'showing', and it celebrates the story of Jesus being shown to the wise men who had travelled to see the new baby king.

Shrove Tuesday Spring
This is the day before the beginning of Lent. It is also known as Pancake Day. People used to make pancakes to use up foods such as fat and eggs that would go off during Lent, when everyone was fasting. Shrove Tuesday is known in many countries by its French name, Mardi Gras, which means 'Fat Tuesday'. It is celebrated with a carnival that sometimes lasts for a week.

Lent Spring
Lent takes place during the six weeks before Easter. It is the time when Christians feel sorry for anything they have done wrong and try to make a new start in their lives. It used to be a time for fasting, and many people still give up something they enjoy eating during Lent.

Good Friday March or April
Good Friday is a very solemn day when Christians remember that Jesus died on the cross.

▲ **Easter Sunday** March or April
Easter is when Christians celebrate Jesus coming back to life again. In many countries, eggs are eaten because they are a symbol of new life. In the Orthodox Church, services are held at midnight as Easter Day begins. The dark church is gradually filled with lighted candles as a symbol that the 'Light of the World' has returned.

Ascension Day May
Ascension Day is forty days after Easter. It is the day when Jesus was last seen on earth.

Pentecost
The Day of Pentecost was the time when Jesus's disciples were given the power of the Holy Spirit to guide them in their work of telling everyone about God. Many Christians hold processions on this day. It is also known as Whit Sunday.

▲ **Harvest Festival** September or October
Churches are decorated with fruit, vegetables and sheaves of corn, as well as flowers, at harvest festival. It is a time when people thank God for the harvest and for providing them with food throughout the year.

GLOSSARY

Bull-roarer A thin, flat, pointed piece of wood attached to a long cord, which is swung above the head to produce a whirring sound.

Castanets Small round wooden instruments that are rattled together in pairs in time with dancing.

Communion An important ceremony in the Christian Church. People share bread and wine, in the way that Jesus and his disciples did at the Last Supper.

Emigrants People who have left one country to settle in another.

Fasting To go without food, or without certain kinds of food.

Fertility To do with the richness of the soil for growing crops; or to do with the reproduction of young or offspring.

Float A platform mounted on a lorry used for a display.

Jazz Lively music of African-American origin.

Moors Muslims who invaded and ruled part of Spain from the eighth century AD. They were finally driven out in 1492 by King Ferdinand and Queen Isabella.

Pancakes Thin flat cakes made of batter, fried and often tossed in the air while cooking.

Percussion Musical instruments that are usually played by being struck with sticks.

Renaissance A time when there were important developments in art and literature, between the fourteenth and sixteenth centuries.

Roman Catholic Belonging to the Christian Church led by the Pope in Rome, Italy.

Slaves People who are legally owned by other people. They have to work without payment for their owners and have no freedom.

BOOKS TO READ

Festivals Around the World by Godfrey Hall (Wayland, 1995)

Nini at Carnival by Errol Lloyd (Bodley Head, 1995)

Winter Festivals by Mike Rosen (Wayland, 1990)

USEFUL ADDRESSES

To find out more about Carnival, you might find these addresses useful:

Commonwealth Institute, Kensington High Street, London W8 6NQ

The Steelband Association of Great Britain, 10 Gainsborough Gardens, Greenford, Middlesex UB6 0JG

High Commission of the Republic of Trinidad and Tobago, 42 Belgrave Square, London SW1X 8NT

The following organizations can give you more information about Christianity:

Catholic Information Service, 74 Gallow Hill Lane, Abbotts Langley, Herts, WD5 0BZ

Church of England Information Office, Church House, Deans Yard, London SW1P 3NZ

Committee for Extra-Diocesan Affairs, Russian Orthodox Cathedral, Ennismore Gardens, London SW7

INDEX